WILD NATURE

ANIMAL GIANTS

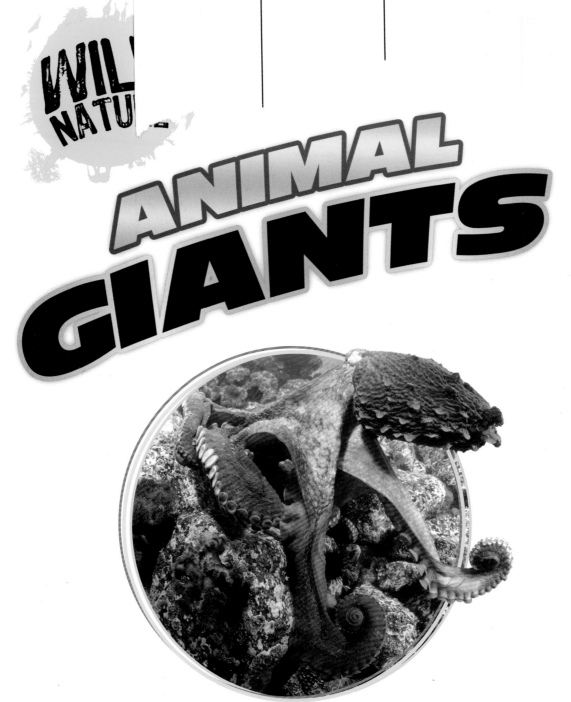

Jinny Johnson

Miles

First published as *My Top 20 Animal Giants* in 2010 by Miles Kelly Publishing Ltd
Harding's Barn, Bardfield End Green, Thaxted, Essex, CM6 3PX, UK

Copyright © Miles Kelly Publishing Ltd 2010

This edition published in 2013

10 9 8 7 6 5 4 3 2 1

Publishing Director Belinda Gallagher
Creative Director Jo Cowan
Editorial Director Rosie McGuire
Senior Editor Claire Philip
Concept Designer Simon Lee
Volume Designer Joe Jones, Rob Hale
Image Manager Liberty Newton
Production Manager Elizabeth Collins
Reprographics Stephan Davis, Thom Allaway

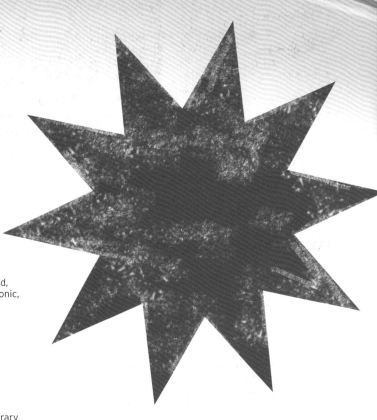

ISBN 978-1-78209-093-9

Printed in China

British Library Cataloguing-in-Publication Data
A catalogue record for this book is available from the British Library

ACKNOWLEDGEMENTS
The publishers would like to thank the following sources for the use of their photographs:
Key: (m) = main (i) = inset

Front cover: (main) Christian Heinrich/Imagebroker/FLPA, (Wild Nature animal globe) ranker/Shutterstock.com
Back cover: (top) Olivier Le Queinec/Shutterstock.com, (bottom) Krysztof Odziomek/Shutterstock.com
Page 1 Boris Pamikov/Shutterstock.com
Pages 4–5 (from left to right) ImageBroker/FLPA, moodboard RF/Photolibrary.com,
Jeffrey L. Rotman/Photolibrary.com; Gerard Soury/Photolibrary.com, Werner Bollmann/Photolibrary.com
African elephant (m) Karl Ammann/naturepl.com, (i) Anup Shah/naturepl.com
Green anaconda (m) Ingo Arndt/Minden Pictures/FLPA, (i) Luiz Claudio Marigo/naturepl.com
Blue whale (m) Flip Nicklin/Minden Pictures/FLPA, (i) Mark Carwardine/naturepl.com
Giant anteater (m) Morales Morales/Photolibrary.com, (i) Pete Oxford/naturepl.com
Galapagos giant tortoise (m) Mark Moffett/Minden Pictures/FLPA (i) Andy Rouse/naturepl.com
Goliath bird-eating spider (m) Rod Williams/naturepl.com
Japanese giant hornet (m) Alastair MacEwen/Photolibrary.com
Giant otter (m) Fritz Polking/FLPA, (i) Luiz Claudio Marigo/naturepl.com
Giant grouper (m) Norbert Wu/Minden Pictures/FLPA, (i) Jurgen Freund/naturepl.com
Hippopotamus (m) Juniors Bildarchiv/Photolibrary.com, (i) Tony Heald/naturepl.com
Komodo dragon (m) R.Dirscherl/FLPA, (i) Reinhard Dirscherl/FLPA
Lion's mane jellyfish (m) Scott Leslie/Minden Pictures/FLPA, (i) ImageBroker/FLPA
Giant coconut crab (m) Ariadne Van Zandbergen/FLPA
Bison (m) ImageBroker/FLPA
Whale shark (m) Andy Rouse/naturepl.com, (i) Jurgen Freund/naturepl.com
Wandering albatross (m) Ben Osborne/Photolibrary.com, (i) Ian McCarthy/naturepl.com
Saltwater crocodile (m) Tom and Pam Gardner/FLPA, (i) Reinhard Dirscherl/FLPA
Manta ray (m) Jens Kuhfs/Getty Images/Photolibrary.com, (i) Brandon Cole/naturepl.com
Giant African land snail (m) Vincent Grafhorst/Minden Pictures/FLPA, (i) Martin B Withers/FLPA
Pacific giant octopus (m) David Fleetham/naturepl.com

Every effort has been made to acknowledge the source and copyright holder of each picture.
Miles Kelly Publishing apologises for any unintentional errors or omissions.

Made with paper from a sustainable forest

www.mileskelly.net   info@mileskelly.net

www.factsforprojects.com

CONTENTS

SUPER-SIZE US: BIG IS BEST

↙ The saltwater crocodile is the largest of its kind, and a very dangerous animal. It catches anything it comes across – even sharks.

Millions of years ago, animal giants such as the dinosaurs *Diplodocus* and *Tyrannosaurus Rex* roamed the Earth. Today there are other monster creatures living on our planet, including the biggest animal ever known – the blue whale.

Being big has advantages. Few animals dare to attack something bigger than themselves, and larger animals are likely to be stronger and able to reach food that others can't. But there are problems too. For example, a big animal needs to find and eat lots of food to have enough energy to survive.

Each animal group has its own giants, but size is relative. A giant hornet is far bigger than any similar species, but tiny compared to an albatross or a giant tortoise.

1

KEEPS YOU SAFE
When you're a giant you have few enemies. Huge and heavy, elephants tower over most other creatures. Even top predators are wary of tackling them for fear of losing the fight.

→ This lion might be on the lookout for a meal, but it won't approach this massive African elephant when it looks like it might charge.

GET LOST

4

2

REACHING FOOD

In the wild, it can be a struggle finding enough to eat. Being big can help you reach food that other animals can't get to, and that's good, because if you're big you need lots of food.

↓ Long arms lined with powerful suckers mean the giant octopus can prey on sharks as well as going after smaller fish.

NEARLY THERE

3

SUPER STRENGTH

Big usually means strong, and this gives giant creatures a huge advantage over their smaller relatives. They can attack with huge power, and greater endurance means they can overcome smaller, weaker prey.

WATCH OUT

↗ With its long neck, the giraffe is the tallest of all animals – up to 6 m – so it can browse on leaves at the very top of trees.

4

TOP PREDATOR

Animals that are very large and equipped with deadly weapons, such as sharp teeth and strong jaws, are able to attack any prey that comes their way. Saltwater crocodiles and killer whales are both top predators.

TIGHT SPOT

→ The killer whale is one of the most powerful of all predators and kills seals, sea lions and sometimes even other whales.

The biggest of all land animals, the African elephant is enormously strong and powerful, but it can be surprisingly gentle too. Despite its great bulk, the elephant can move around almost silently and caresses its young with a soothing stroke of its trunk. But when frightened or angry, an elephant will bulldoze anything in its path while making loud trumpeting calls. Both male and female African elephants have huge tusks, which they use for digging up food and stripping bark from trees to eat.

TRUNK AND TUSKS

BIG BABIES...

ON GUARD...

Elephant mums stay close to their young. Few predators dare to attack a baby elephant when mum, her giant tusks at the ready, is standing guard.

A newborn baby elephant can weigh as much as 120 kg – more than 30 times the weight of an average human baby – and is 1 m tall.

SPECIAL FEATURES

TRUNK: An elephant's trunk is its nose and upper lip all in one. It is used for smelling, drinking and lifting and is terrifically strong.

EARS: An elephant flaps its big ears to help cool itself down. It also flaps its ears when calling or listening to other elephants' calls.

African elephant

Scientific name: *Loxodonta africana*
Type: Mammal
Lifespan: About 60 years
Height: Male up to 4 m, female 3.4 m
Weight: Male up to 6.3 tonnes, female 3.5 tonnes
Range: Africa, south of the Sahara
Status: Near threatened

STAR FACT

An African elephant's tusks are actually very long front teeth. A male's tusks can be 2 m in length and each one can weigh more than 60 kg — that's as much as an adult human!

FEET: An elephant's foot is like a big, spongy cushion with the toes buried inside. This shape helps spread the elephant's great weight.

APPETITE: A big elephant needs lots of food, munching through more than 150 kg of leaves, twigs, roots and fruit every day.

A few snake species beat the anaconda on length, but this snake's chunky coils make it the heaviest of all. It can weigh as much as three humans and grow longer than two cars parked end-to-end. Lurking in shallow water or on the forest floor, the anaconda waits for prey such as capybaras (giant rodents), peccaries (mammals similar to wild pigs) and caimans (alligator-like reptiles). When one wanders near, the snake seizes it, wraps its coils around its struggling body, and squeezes so tightly that the prey suffocates.

COLOSSAL COILS

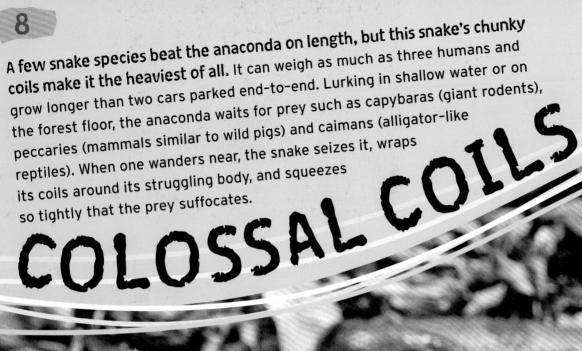

'STAR FACT

It can take an anaconda around six hours to swallow a large animal such as a capybara, which weighs around 45 kg. But after that, the snake won't need another meal for several months.

SPECIAL FEATURES

ADAPTATIONS: Eyes and nostrils positioned right on top of the head allow the anaconda to breathe and keep watch for prey while in water.

WIDE MOUTH: Stretchy jaws mean that the anaconda can open its mouth super wide, allowing it to swallow prey larger than its own head.

Green anaconda

Scientific name: *Eunectes murinus*
Type: Reptile
Lifespan: 10 years, rarely up to 25
Length: 6–10 m, female longer and heavier than male
Weight: Up to 225 kg
Range: Northern South America
Status: Least concern

SHHHH...

Despite its huge size, the anaconda's mottled colouration makes it hard to spot among dead leaves on the forest floor.

A full-grown anaconda can measure as much as 30 cm around its body – thicker than an adult man's arm.

GREAT LENGTHS...

SWIMMING: An excellent swimmer, the anaconda is able to hunt its prey in water just as expertly as it does on land.

GROWTH: From birth to full maturity an anaconda will increase about 500 times in weight – more than any other snake species.

The blue whale is the biggest animal ever to have lived on our planet – twice the size of the largest dinosaur. This gigantic creature spends all its life in the sea feeding on tiny shrimp-like animals called krill, which it filters from the water. It may eat 3.5 tonnes – about 40 million – of these in a day. Even a newborn baby blue whale is huge, weighing more than a full-grown hippo. It drinks 400 litres of its mother's milk every day – that's about two big bathtubs full!

BIGGEST OF ALL

CRASH...

A blue whale prepares to dive, raising its huge tail, measuring 7.5 m across, above the water. The whale can dive down to 500 m.

SPECIAL FEATURES

HEART: The blue whale's heart weighs as much as a small car – it has to be big to pump blood through the whale's massive body.

BALEEN PLATES: The whale filters food through plates of fringed material called baleen hanging from its upper jaws.

AWESOME...

A mighty blue whale dwarfs this 7-m-long research boat. The whale can swim as fast as an ocean liner, at up to 48 km/h.

Blue whale

Scientific name: *Balaenoptera musculus*
Type: Mammal
Lifespan: 80 years, sometimes 100-plus
Length: 25–32 m
Weight: 180 tonnes, female usually heavier than male
Range: Oceans worldwide
Status: Endangered

'STAR FACT

Not only are blue whales the biggest of all animals, they are also among the loudest. They make a wide range of sounds, which can be heard by other blue whales more than 1500 km away.

TONGUE: The tongue of a blue whale weighs at least 2.7 tonnes – as much as an elephant. The whale uses it to push water out of its mouth and krill down its throat.

STREAMLINED BODY: The whale's sleek, tapering shape helps it to move through the water gracefully at high speed.

The biggest of its kind, the giant anteater is a large, powerful animal – but its prey is surprisingly tiny. It eats only ants and termites, tearing open their nests with its strong front feet. The anteater won't destroy the nests completely or kill all the termites because it knows that if it allows the insects to repair their home, it will be able to come back again and again for more meals. Although not an aggressive animal, the giant anteater can wound an attacker with its long claws.

TERMITE TASTER

GREEDY...

An anteater needs a lot of termites or ants to make a meal. It eats as many as 30,000 of these little insects every day!

SPECIAL FEATURES

NOSE AND EARS: The giant anteater tracks down insect nests with the help of its keen sense of smell and good hearing. Its eyesight is poor.

STRONG STOMACH: This mammal has a strong stomach and special digestive juices to break down the tough little creatures it feeds on.

Giant anteater

Scientific name: *Myrmecophaga tridactyla*
Type: Mammal
Lifespan: About 14 years
Length: Head-body 1–2 m, tail up to 90 cm
Weight: 22–39 kg
Range: Central and South America
Status: Near threatened

WEIRD...

The giant anteater is perfectly adapted for its life as one of the most specialized of all insect eaters, with its slender, tapering snout and long, sharp claws.

STAR FACT

This anteater's tongue is 60 cm in length, and covered in tiny spines and sticky saliva. The anteater can flick its tongue out 160 times every minute to gobble up its scurrying insect prey.

SKIN AND HAIR: Long hair and thick skin help to protect the anteater from the bites of termites and ants as they try to defend their nests.

SHARP CLAWS: The claws on a giant anteater's front feet are up to 10 cm in length and very strong – ideal for tearing open termite nests.

The enormous Galapagos tortoise weighs more than four adult humans. It is one of the world's largest tortoises, and one of the biggest of all reptiles. Its massive shell is made of bone, and it can draw its soft head and limbs in underneath it to protect itself. A peaceful and slow-moving creature, the Galapagos tortoise spends a few hours every morning basking in the sunshine to warm itself up and then rambles around feeding on grass, leaves and flowers. It sleeps for at least 14 hours at night.

STAR FACT

This giant is friendly with finches. The birds pick off and eat ticks from the tortoise's folds of skin. The bird gets a meal and the tortoise gets a break from the itchy parasites.

BONY SHELL

LAZY BATHERS...

Galapagos tortoises like water and will bask and even sleep in muddy pools and puddles.

SPECIAL FEATURES

WATER STORES: This tortoise can survive for a year without food or drink, thanks to its very slow systems and its ability to store water in its body.

SENSE OF SMELL: Like other land tortoises, the Galapagos tortoise has a good sense of smell which helps it track down plants to eat.

Galapagos giant tortoise

Scientific name: *Geochelone elephantopus*
Type: Reptile
Lifespan: 100–150 years
Length: Up to 1.2 m
Weight: 300 kg
Range: Galapagos Islands
Status: Vulnerable

YUMMY...

Tortoises that feed on the ground have domed shells, but those that stretch up to feed on higher plants have shells that curve in at the front so that they can lift their heads.

SERRATED JAWS: The lower jaws have tough ridges with serrated (saw-like) edges. These allow the tortoise to bite through cactus stems and other tough plants.

LEGS AND FEET: Short, thick legs shaped like pillars support the Galapagos tortoise's great weight. Its feet are equipped with strong claws to help it dig.

The largest of all spiders, this creepy-crawly has a chunky body and four pairs of long hairy legs. Despite its name, it doesn't usually eat birds, but hunts large insects, lizards and even mice, killing them by biting with its poisonous fangs. Usually active at night, it spends its days sheltering in a silk-lined burrow dug into the ground or under leaves on the forest floor. The female is bigger than the male and will sometimes eat her partner after mating.

HAIRY HORROR

Goliath bird-eating spider

Scientific name: *Theraphosa blondi*
Type: Arachnid
Lifespan: Males 3–6 years, females 10–12 years
Legspan: 30 cm
Weight: 170 g
Range: Northern South America
Status: Not enough information

POUNCE...

This spider is a stealth hunter, pouncing on victims and paralyzing them with its venomous bite, then breaking their flesh down with special digestive juices.

STAR FACT

If disturbed, this spider can make a loud hissing sound by rubbing the bristles on its legs together to warn off the enemy. This sound can be heard more than 4 m away.

SPECIAL FEATURES

FANGS: This spider's fangs are 2.5 cm in length and linked to poison glands. A bite is not fatal for humans but is very painful.

HAIRS: The body is covered with tiny hairs that the spider can flick off at an attacker. These can cause swelling and irritation.

SUPER STINGER

The world's largest wasp, the Japanese giant hornet is a dangerous and aggressive insect. It preys on other insects and can kill a whole colony of bees in just a few hours. The hornets don't actually eat the bees – they chew them up to feed to their larvae. The adult hornets then drink a saliva made by the larvae that is said to provide them with amazing energy. They can fly nearly 100 kilometres in a day at speeds of up to 40 kilometres an hour.

STRIKE...

This hornet can kill 40 honeybees in a minute. In Japan it kills more people every year than any other animal, including snakes.

Japanese giant hornet

Scientific name: *Vespa mandarinia*
Type: Insect
Lifespan: Probably several months
Length: 5 cm
Wingspan: Up to 7.5 cm
Range: Eastern Asia
Status: Least concern

STAR FACT

In Japan, they make a drink called hornet juice based on the saliva made by hornet larvae. This miracle drink is said to boost the performance of athletes.

SPECIAL FEATURES

STING: The hornet has a 6 mm sting that it drives into its prey to inject its venom, and which can be used over and over again.

VENOM: The giant hornet's venom contains a chemical substance strong enough to dissolve human tissue.

The giant otter spends much of its life in rivers and streams and is an expert swimmer and diver. In South America, where these otters live, they are known as 'wolves of the river' and just like real wolves they live and hunt in family groups. Each otter family makes a large den in a riverbank. Here the breeding pair rear their young, defending their home and territory fiercely if an enemy dares to come near.

WEBBED WONDER

TASTY...

Fish, such as piranhas, are this predator's main food and the otter may eat several kilograms of fish every day. It also catches crabs and even snakes.

SPECIAL FEATURES

THICK FUR: The giant otter's very thick, dense fur is water repellent, helping to keep the animal warm and dry.

FEET AND TAIL: Large webbed feet and a long, very muscular tail help make the otter an agile, powerful swimmer.

Giant otter

Scientific name: *Pteroneura brasiliensis*
Type: Mammal
Lifespan: 8–10 years
Length: Head-body 1–1.4 m, tail up to 65 cm
Weight: Males up to 34 kg, females up to 26 kg
Range: Northern South America
Status: Endangered

The giant otter moves more awkwardly on land than in water, but still manages to travel long distances between rivers and lakes.

GETTING AROUND…

SPECIAL EARS: The giant otter is able to close off its ears when it dives for food to prevent water from getting inside them.

WHISKERS: The long whiskers are highly sensitive to touch, helping the otter to find prey in muddy or sandy water where visibility is poor.

Longer than an adult human, the giant grouper is a highly aggressive fish and weighs almost as much as two people. It feeds on other fish as well as on crustaceans such as lobsters and crabs, and defends its territory and feeding grounds fiercely. Although this giant is a member of the grouper family, it is also known as the potato cod because of the irregular oval markings on its body. It is one of a number of large groupers, all of which are prized as food fish.

FIERCE FISH

SURPRISE...

The giant grouper lives around coral reefs where it is usually the largest of the inhabitants. It hides among the coral and ambushes any prey that swims past.

STAR FACT

Most groupers start life as females, and become male when they have grown to about 12 kg in weight. If there are no males in an area, a female becomes male sooner.

SPECIAL FEATURES

BIG MOUTH: Like all groupers, this fish has a very large mouth than can engulf any unwary prey that comes within range.

SHARP TEETH: Some of the teeth at the front of the jaw face inwards, making it tricky for prey to escape once they are inside the grouper's mouth.

Giant grouper

Scientific name: *Epinephelus tukula*
Type: Fish
Lifespan: Up to 50 years
Length: Up to 2 m
Weight: 110 kg
Range: Tropical and subtropical waters of the Indian Ocean and western Pacific Ocean
Status: Least concern

BACK OFF...

Giant groupers are inquisitive fish and often swim up to investigate divers. However it's best not to get too close, as they can be dangerous.

CAMOUFLAGE: The irregular dark markings on the grouper's body help it to stay hidden among the rocks and coral as it lies in wait for unwary prey.

COLOUR CHANGE: Groupers can change colour from dark to light to match their surroundings and make their camouflage even more effective.

The huge, bulky-bodied hippopotamus spends most of its time wallowing in lakes or rivers to keep cool. Despite its less-than-agile build it is a surprisingly good swimmer, but it's so big that it can often walk along the river or lake bed rather than swim. At night, hippos haul themselves out of the water onto land where they feed on massive quantities of grass. They live in groups of about 15 or so females and young, led by an adult male, but may sometimes gather in large herds of up to 150 animals.

BARREL BODY

A newborn hippo weighs up to 50 kg – more than an average 12-year-old child. It swims before it can walk and feeds on its mother's milk underwater.

AAHH...

SPECIAL FEATURES

NATURAL MOISTURE: The hippo's thick skin contains an oily substance. This acts like a natural sunblock, and prevents the skin from cracking.

EYES AND NOSE: Nostrils and eyes are set high on the hippo's head so it can see and breathe when lying almost submerged in water.

STAR FACT

The hippopotamus is the third largest land mammal after the elephant and white rhino. Despite its great size, it is a fast runner and can sprint along at more than 30 km/h.

Hippopotamus

Scientific name: *Hippopotamus amphibius*
Type: Mammal
Lifespan: Up to 40 years
Length: Head-body up to 5 m, tail 50 cm
Weight: Up to 4.5 tonnes
Range: Parts of Africa south of the Sahara
Status: Vulnerable

OUCH...

Male hippos can be highly aggressive, battling with each other over territory and females.

SCENT MARKING: Hippos mark their territory by leaving heaps of dung on the river bank and may even spread it around with their tails to warn off enemies.

MOUTH AND TEETH: The mouth measures up to 1.2 m across. The lower canine teeth are 30 cm long and weigh as much as 3 kg – equal to three bags of sugar.

The largest, heaviest lizard on Earth, the Komodo dragon looks like a creature that belongs to the age of dinosaurs. This fierce predator is armed with sharp claws and large, jagged teeth, and will eat almost anything it can catch, from deer and pigs to much larger animals such as water buffalo. Very little is wasted and the dragons will even eat bones, hooves and skin. They will also scavenge carrion (animals that are already dead). Like many reptiles, Komodos reproduce by laying eggs.

DEADLY LIZARD

GROSS....

Komodos eat up to 80 percent of their own body weight in a single meal, and will happily feast on dead marine animals such as dolphins that wash up on the shore of their island home.

SPECIAL FEATURES

TONGUE: The dragon's tongue flicks in and out constantly, analyzing the air for the scent of prey. It can detect a dead animal from over 8 km away.

TEETH: A Komodo dragon has more than 60 teeth, each up to 2.5 cm in length. The teeth have serrated edges like those of sharks.

LOOK OUT...

Despite its bulky shape and short stocky legs, the Komodo is a fast mover and can run at speeds of up to 18 km/h over short distances as it chases its prey. It is also a good swimmer.

Komodo dragon

Scientific name: *Varanus komodoensis*
Type: Reptile
Lifespan: About 30 years
Length: 3 m
Weight: 150 kg
Range: Lesser Sunda Islands, Indonesia
Status: Vulnerable

'STAR FACT

Venom glands in the Komodo's jaws mean that if it bites a victim that then escapes, the dragon just has to follow its prey and wait. In 24 hours the wounded animal will die from the effects of the poison.

FLEXIBLE JAWS: To enable it to tear off and swallow large pieces of flesh, the Komodo has a huge mouth and powerful, flexible jaws.

TAIL: The dragon's tail is as long as its body and very heavy. It can use it as a support when standing up on its hind legs to reach prey.

Can you imagine a jellyfish with a body bigger than a double bed and trailing tentacles longer than a bus? That is about the size of the lion's mane jellyfish, the largest known of its kind. This amazing creature gets its name from its mass of thin, hairlike tentacles, which it uses for capturing prey such as small fish and shellfish. They are most common in cold waters and the biggest specimens are found in the Arctic Ocean.

TERRIBLE TENTACLES

STAR FACT

A jellyfish's body actually consists of around 95 percent water, and although they are animals, they have no bones, blood or brain!

WHOA...

The biggest ever lion's mane jellyfish is said to have had tentacles longer than a blue whale, the largest animal in the world.

SPECIAL FEATURES

STINGING CELLS: The jellyfish's super-long tentacles are lined with stinging cells that release barbed stingers upon contact, paralyzing prey.

BELL: A jellyfish's saucer-shaped body is called a bell, and its mouth is located at the centre of the underside of the bell.

Lion's mane jellyfish

Scientific name: *Cyanea capillata*
Type: Cnidarian
Lifespan: About 1 year
Length: Bell up to 2 m across, tentacles 30 m-plus
Weight: 200 kg
Range: Arctic and cooler waters of Atlantic and Pacific oceans
Status: Not enough information

The jellyfish's stinging cells can be very dangerous to humans and cause painful wounds so if you see one, stay well clear!

DON'T TOUCH...

TENTACLES: The extraordinarily long tentacles of this jellyfish are grouped in eight clusters, with each cluster containing about 150 tentacles.

ORAL ARMS: As well as its tentacles, the lion's mane jellyfish also has special arms called oral arms for carrying food to its mouth.

The largest of all land crabs, the spectacular coconut crab is a kind of hermit crab, so it does not have a hard shell. A young coconut crab shelters in a discarded snail shell, but when it gets too big for this it grows a tough, protective skin over its body. This crab is so well adapted to life on land that it has lost the ability to swim. Coconuts are its main food, but it also eats other fruits and leaves and will gobble up the discarded shells of other crustaceans.

MEGA PINCERS

Giant coconut crab

Scientific name: *Birgus latro*
Type: Crustacean
Lifespan: Up to 40 years
Legspan: 1 m
Weight: 3 kg
Range: Islands in the Indian and Pacific oceans
Status: Not enough information

'STAR FACT'

This giant crab is so strong that it can lift objects such as rocks or branches that weigh as much as 28 kg – the weight of an average eight- or nine-year-old child!

SCUTTLE...

These crabs climb coconut palms with ease and are able to open coconut shells with their huge claws to get at the flesh inside.

SPECIAL FEATURES

TEN LEGS: This crab has five pairs of legs. The front pair is not used for walking and bears huge claws for breaking open its food.

SENSE OF SMELL: Coconut crabs are able to pick up the scent of food such as coconuts and bananas over long distances.

HEAVY HULK

The bison, also known as the American buffalo, is the largest, heaviest land animal in North America. This impressive beast has a massive head, bulky shoulders and shaggy fur. Males and females generally live in separate herds, roaming the plains and feeding on grasses and shrubs. They come together in the mating season when rival males may battle with one another for the right to mate with females.

ZOOM...

Despite their size, bison are surprisingly fast runners, speeding along at up to 65 km/h to escape predators such as wolves.

STAR FACT

There were millions of bison in North America, but in the late 19th century they were hunted nearly to extinction. Now the numbers are rising again and there are about 200,000.

Bison

Scientific name: *Bison bison*
Type: Mammal
Lifespan: 12–20 years
Length: Head-body up to 3.5 m, tail 60 cm
Weight: Up to 1000 kg
Range: North America
Status: Near threatened

SPECIAL FEATURES

THICK COAT: The bison's long and shaggy coat keeps it warm during the harsh winters on the prairie. It sheds some hair in spring.

HORNS: The huge horns are up to 61 cm in length. They are made of bone and covered with keratin – the same substance as human fingernails.

The biggest shark species and the biggest of all fish, the mighty whale shark can grow to be longer than a bus and weighs as much as eight or nine cars. Although monstrous in size, this fish is harmless to humans, feeding only on planktonic creatures that it filters from the water. It has a wide head and a massive body that tapers towards a large crescent-shaped tail. It patrols the oceans slowly, usually only at speeds of around 5 kilometres an hour.

MONSTER MOUTH

SUPER-SIZED...

Unsurprisingly, this whale shark dwarfs a nearby human diver – these fish can grow to at least eight times the length of an average adult human.

SPECIAL FEATURES

PATTERN: Whale sharks' bodies have patterns of light spots and stripes on dark backgrounds, making this species instantly recognizable.

TEETH: There are about 300 teeth in each of the whale shark's jaws, but these don't seem to be used for feeding. Each is only 3 mm in length.

Whale shark

Scientific name: *Rhincodon typus*
Type: Fish
Lifespan: 60–100 years
Length: 15 m, rarely up to 20 m
Weight: 18.5 tonnes
Range: Tropical and warm temperate seas (not Mediterranean)
Status: Vulnerable

SLURP...

The whale shark's gaping mouth sucks in water containing tiny plankton and small fish. Sieve-like structures on its gills filter the creatures from the water so the shark can swallow them.

TOUGH SKIN: Like all sharks, a whale shark's skin is covered with tiny, tooth-like structures called denticles, which feel like sandpaper and provide protection.

WIDE MOUTH: The mouth is very wide and located on the front of the head, allowing the shark to take in large amounts of water when filtering food.

The majestic wandering albatross has the largest wingspan of any bird. From tip to tip the wings measure an amazing 3.4 metres – as much as a small car. The albatross spends most of its life in flight, gliding on air currents over the sea. The wind does most of the work, so the bird hardly needs to beat its massive wings. It lands on the sea only to feed and usually just dips its head and beak below the surface to snatch fish or squid.

HIGH FLIER

SQUAWK...

This albatross rarely comes to land except to breed. The female lays only one egg and the parents care for their chick for about nine months.

SPECIAL FEATURES

HOOKED BEAK: The strong beak, with its sharp edges and hooked tip, is ideally shaped for catching slippery fish and tearing them apart.

SENSE OF SMELL: Unlike many birds, albatrosses have a good sense of smell, and can scent floating carrion from several kilometres away.

Wandering albatross

Scientific name: *Diomedea exulans*
Type: Bird
Lifespan: 30 years
Length: 1.1 m
Weight: 8–11.5 kg
Range: Southern oceans
Status: Vulnerable

STAR FACT

Albatrosses are capable of flying huge distances. One bird was tracked travelling 6000 km over the course of only 12 days – that's 500 km every day.

FOLLOW THAT FOOD...

Albatrosses often follow fishing boats, swooping down to feed on the scraps that get thrown overboard.

WEBBED FEET: The albatross uses its large webbed feet for paddling when on the water's surface and as brakes when in flight.

SALT GLANDS: Special glands near the eyes help remove the salt that builds up in the albatross' body from its prey and sea water.

At least twice the length of an adult human, the saltwater crocodile is the biggest of all croc species. It is a fierce predator and lurks in shallow water where it watches and waits for prey. If a potential victim such as a buffalo, monkey or wild boar ventures near the water's edge, the crocodile lunges with surprising speed and seizes the animal in its huge jaws. It then drags its catch back to the water and pulls it under the surface. Once the creature has drowned, the saltie can feed, biting off large chunks of flesh.

ARMOURED HUNTER

A young saltwater crocodile opens its huge gaping jaws wide, ready to attack its prey.

OPEN WIDE...

SPECIAL FEATURES

STRONG TAIL: When swimming, the crocodile moves its strong tail from side to side, holding its legs close to its sides.

EARS AND NOSE: The eyes and nostrils are high on the head, so the croc can breathe and watch out for prey while lying almost submerged in water.

MOVE IT...

On land the crocodile can wriggle along on its tummy, pushing with its feet, or lift itself up off the ground to move more rapidly.

Saltwater crocodile

Scientific name: *Crocodylus porosus*
Type: Reptile
Lifespan: About 70 years
Length: 6 m
Weight: 450 kg
Range: Southeast Asia, northern Australia
Status: Least concern

STAR FACT

Female crocs lay eggs in nests made from mounds of plant matter and mud. If the nest temperature is about 31.5°C the hatchlings will be males. If it is warmer or cooler they will be females.

TEETH: The crocodile's long, powerful jaws house up to 68 sharp teeth, which help it to quickly tear even large prey into chunks small enough to swallow.

BODY ARMOUR: Embedded in the thick skin on the crocodile's back are pieces of bone that help to protect it from the bites and scratches of struggling prey.

Like a huge underwater bird, the manta ray moves through the surface waters of the ocean by flapping its enormous winglike fins. Although it is the largest of the rays and a close relative of sharks it is not a fierce hunter, instead feeding on small planktonic creatures (microscopic animals and plants), which it filters from the water through special spongy plates on its gills. A manta ray may eat more than 17 kilograms of its tiny prey every day.

WINGED SWIMMER

GULP...

The ray uses the long lobes on either side of its head to funnel water into its mouth. Small fish and plankton become trapped on the manta's gill plates while the water flows out again.

SPECIAL FEATURES

CARTILAGE: Like other rays and sharks, the manta's skeleton is made of cartilage (a tough, gristly material), making its 'wings' very flexible.

SPECIAL HELPERS: Small fish such as wrasse help mantas by removing parasites and cleaning any wounds on their bodies.

Manta ray

Scientific name: *Manta birostris*
Type: Fish
Lifespan: About 20 years
Width: Up to 7 m
Weight: Up to 1.3 tonnes
Range: Temperate, subtropical and tropical waters worldwide
Status: Near threatened

'STAR 'FACT

The manta ray makes regular migrations (seasonal journeys) across the Indian Ocean. One ray was tracked travelling an incredible 1100 km in just 60 days.

SPLASH...

The manta is a graceful swimmer and will sometimes make spectacular leaps above the water's surface.

TEETH: Inside its huge, cavernous mouth the manta has 18 rows of small teeth on its lower jaw, but these are not used for trapping food.

COLOURATION: The underside of the body is pale with dark blotches. The pattern is different in every manta and can be used to identify individuals.

This monster mollusc is the world's largest land snail. It comes from East Africa and has now spread to many other tropical areas. A big eater, it chomps its way through large amounts of almost any plants it can find – including food crops, so it is generally considered to be a pest. Like many snails, this giant is usually active at night and spends its days buried in damp earth. It stays underground during long dry periods too, until rain tempts it out into the open air again.

SUPER SLITHERER

WOW...

On the snail's head are two sets of tentacles. The longer pair carry its eyes and the shorter set help the snail to touch and smell.

STAR FACT

In 1966 an American boy brought three of these snails back from Hawaii to Florida, USA and let them loose in his garden. Seven years later there were more than 18,000 of these snails in the state.

TAKE ME HOME...

This snail is as big as an adult human's hand. Some people like them so much that they keep them as pets.

SPECIAL FEATURES

SHELL: Like all snails, this giant can pull its vulnerable soft body into its hard outer shell to protect itself from predators.

SLIME: The snail moves along on its large flattened body, called a foot. The foot gives off slime, which helps the snail to slither along.

Giant African land snail

Scientific name: *Achatina fulica*
Type: Mollusc
Lifespan: Up to 9 years
Length: Shell up to 20 cm, extended body up to 30 cm
Weight: Up to 450 g
Range: East Africa, but has been introduced to many other tropical areas
Status: Least concern

ROUGH TONGUE: A tongue-like structure covered with lots of tiny toothlike spikes helps the snail scrape up its food.

FAST BREEDER: This snail lays five or six batches of as many as 200 eggs each year. Most of the babies survive so the species spreads fast.

The world's largest octopus spends its time lurking among rocks below the water's surface. Concealed in the murky shadows it watches for prey such as crabs and scallops, which it then pulls apart with its strong, sucker-lined arms. The arms are linked to a rounded structure called the mantle, which is actually its head and body combined. Octopuses are thought to be the most intelligent of all invertebrates (animals without backbones).

ARMED AND READY

Pacific giant octopus

Scientific name: Octopus dofleini
Type: Mollusc
Lifespan: About 4 years
Length: 5 m
Weight: 40 kg on average but largest recorded was 272 kg
Range: Pacific coast of North America
Status: Not assessed

WHOOSH...

Like all octopuses, this giant swims by jet propulsion. It sucks water into the web of skin at the base of its arms then quickly expels it to push itself forwards at speed.

'STAR FACT

When resting, the octopus' colour matches its surroundings. But when angry or alarmed it can change to brighter colours to warn off enemies or scare away rivals.

SPECIAL FEATURES

EIGHT ARMS: The arms are lined with two rows of suction cups. There are about 260 cups on each arm, which help the octopus hold onto prey.

EYES: An octopus has very large eyes and excellent eyesight. Its eyes are very similar in structure to human eyes.